WOR█████████

For

A Return to Love

Reflections on the Principles of

"A Course in Miracles"

A Guide to Marianne Williamson's Book

QuantumInk Publications

Table of content

How to Use This Workbook

Welcome to the workbook designed by **QuantumInk Publications** to enhance your understanding and experience of "A Return to Love: Reflections on the Principles of 'A Course in Miracles" by Marianne Williamson. This workbook is designed to help you delve deeper into the teachings and principles presented in the book and apply them to your own life. Here's how you can make the most of this workbook:

1. Read the Book First:

Before using this workbook, it's important to read the main book, "A Return to Love." This will provide you with the foundational knowledge necessary to fully engage with the workbook exercises.

2. Create a Reflective Space:

This will help you connect with the teachings on a deeper level.

3. Set Your Intention:

Before beginning each session, take a moment to set an intention. Ask yourself what you hope to gain from this practice and how you'd like to grow through the teachings.

4. Session Structure:

Each session in the workbook corresponds to a specific chapter or theme from "A Return to Love." Follow this structure for effective practice:

a. Review:

Start by briefly reviewing the main concepts from the relevant chapter in the main book. Refresh your memory on the teachings and insights presented.

b. Reflection:

Read the questions and prompts provided in the workbook for the corresponding chapter. Take your time to contemplate and journal your thoughts and feelings in response to these prompts. Don't rush; allow your inner thoughts to flow freely.

c. Application:

Think about how you can apply the teachings to your daily life. Consider specific situations where the principles could make a positive impact. Write down action steps you can take to integrate these principles.

d. Affirmations:

Affirmations can reinforce positive beliefs and attitudes. Create personal affirmations based on the teachings of the chapter. Write them down and repeat them regularly.

e. Gratitude:

End each session with a gratitude practice. Reflect on the insights gained from the chapter and the workbook exercises.

5. Consistency Matters:

Consistency is key to internalizing the teachings. Set aside dedicated time for your workbook practice—

whether it's daily, weekly, or at your preferred interval—and stick to it.

6. Share and Discuss:

Consider joining a study group or discussing your insights with friends who have also read the book. Engaging in conversations can offer new perspectives and deepen your understanding.

7. Be Patient with Yourself:

Personal growth is a journey. The teachings in the book and this workbook are meant to be a guide for gradual transformation.

8. Celebrate Progress:

Periodically review your journal entries and affirmations to see how far you've come. Celebrate your progress and acknowledge the positive changes you've made in your life.

The main book's synopsis

Marianne Williamson is the author of the book "A Return to Love: Reflections on the Principles of 'A Course in Miracles'". In "A Course in Miracles," a self-study spiritual manual that gives a special viewpoint on forgiveness, love, and personal development, the spiritual principles are presented with a modern interpretation.

The book discusses how fear frequently prevents people from reaching their full potential and emphasizes the strength of love as the supreme force in the universe. According to Marianne Williamson, embracing love and letting go of fear can result in significant personal development and spiritual enlightenment. She explores ideas like forgiving, the ego's contribution to pain, and the value of developing a loving outlook in all facets of life.

Williamson exhorts readers to exercise forgiveness—not just for others but also for themselves—and to view the world through the eyes of love. She talks about how people can find healing when they align with the values of love and acknowledge their innate worth.

In conclusion, "A Return to Love" is a manual for putting "A Course in Miracles" principles into practice to promote personal development, strengthen bonds with others, and live a more satisfying life by letting go of fear and accepting the healing power of love.

Part I: Principles

1. Hell

Educative lessons:

- Lesson on the Nature of Evil and Choice: "Hell" is frequently thought of as a place where evildoers go once they die. This idea calls into question the existence of evil, free will, and the effects of our decisions.

- Divine Accountability and Judgment: Lesson The idea of "hell" emphasizes the notion of divine judgment, in which people are held accountable for the deeds and intents they committed while living on earth.

- Redemption and Free Will: Lesson The idea of "hell" emphasizes the value of free choice and the ability to make the right decision between good and evil. It inspires reflection on the likelihood of salvation and the significance of repentance.

- Lesson: Theology of Mercy and Forgiveness Discussions on "hell" frequently inspire thoughts about God's forgiveness and mercy.
- It's a chance to consider how ideas of divine justice interact with ideas of the love and compassion that are inherent in the divine.
- Lesson: Moral and ethical reflection the idea of "hell" inspires people to consider their moral and ethical decisions. It inspires ideas for leading a moral life, atoning for wrongs, and pursuing transformation.
- Lesson on Spiritual Development and Transformation: The concept of "hell" encourages reflection on the ability of spirituality to improve one's life and the possibility of turning away from negativity, sin, and harmful habits and onto a path of development and enlightenment.

Food for thought:

The Power of Choice: Consider the enormous responsibility that comes with your decisions. How does the idea of "hell" serve as a reminder to you of the value of acting by your moral principles given that you can choose between doing good and doing harm?

_____

_____

_____

_____

_____

_____

Consider your responsibility for your conduct as you face consequences. How does the concept of "hell" motivate you to think about the implications of your decisions and how they might affect your spiritual development?

_____

_____

_____

_____

_____

_____

Investigate the interaction between divine mercy and justice. How can you balance these characteristics within your conception of "hell," taking into account God's mercy and the necessity of responsibility?

_____

_____

_____

_____

_____

_____

Consider the possibility of transformation and renewal when practicing transformative repentance. What reflections about your capacity to ask for forgiveness, make amends, and advance spiritually through repentance could be sparked by the idea of "hell"?

Consider the significance of leading a good life. How does thinking about "hell" motivate you to pursue goodness, kindness, and moral conduct in your dealings with people and in your larger life decisions?

_____

_____

_____

_____

_____

_____

The Path to Light: Consider the difference between darkness and light. How does the idea of "hell" inspire you to think about how you've changed from negativity to positivity, from damaging habits to a more enlightened course?

_____

_____

_____

_____

_____

_____

Accepting Transformation: Consider the concept of spiritual development. How can the idea of "hell" motivate you to value personal development and transformation, realizing that your experiences in life have the power to shape and mold you into the person you are today?

_____

_____

_____

_____

_____

_____

2. God

Educative lessons:

- Explore the idea that "God" isn't necessarily a remote divinity but rather a presence that exists within you and all of creation, serving to remind you of your innate connection to the divine.

- Unconditional Love: Consider the notion that the very nature of "God" is frequently equated with unrestricted love. As examples of divine qualities, this lesson exhorts you to put compassion, forgiveness, and acceptance into practice.

- Consider how the idea of "God" might encourage you to transcend constraints and develop a sense of infinite possibility, encouraging you to draw on your inner fortitude and bravery.

- Find out more about the idea of unity and oneness that "God" represents. Consider how all living things are interconnected and how realizing this connectivity might promote greater compassion and harmony.

- Think about the importance of believing in a greater design and divine order. This knowledge might provide you solace in trying times by serving as a reminder that something bigger is developing.

- Consider the idea of seeking inner guidance from the spiritual source that resides inside you. You are urged by this lesson to develop your intuition, inner wisdom, and closer ties to the divine.

Food for thought:

Consider the notion that you have a link to the divine within you. How can thinking about "God" help you to recognize and maintain this inner connection, enabling you to draw on a reservoir of knowledge and direction?

_____

_____

_____

_____

_____

_____

Consider how the idea of "God" represents the unconditional nature of love. How may this encourage you to prioritize love in all of your interactions, connections, and decisions such that it reflects the divine essence that you possess?

_____

_____

_____

_____

_____

_____

Overcoming Limitations: Consider the significance of overcoming restrictions. How does looking into the idea of "God" inspire you to overcome obstacles and your worries and lead you to experience more empowerment?

_____

_____

_____

_____

_____

_____

Think about how all life is interconnected and the concept of unity among all beings. How may your perception of "God" as a uniting power inspire you to see everyone as a manifestation of this heavenly unity, therefore promoting compassion and understanding?

_____

_____

_____

_____

_____

_____

Faith in Divine Order: Think about what we can learn from having faith in divine order. How can thinking about "God" help you submit to a greater design and traverse the uncertainties of life with a sense of serenity and purpose?

_____

_____

_____

_____

_____

_____

Advice from Within: Consider asking your inner heavenly source for advice. How does the idea of "God" encourage you to follow your instincts, realizing that solutions and revelations frequently come from a closer connection to the divine within you?

_____

_____

_____

_____

_____

_____

Consider the thought of accepting a higher purpose as you consider adopting the Divine Plan. How may thinking about "God" motivate you to conform your activities to a higher purpose, encouraging you to make a beneficial impact on the world and live by the divine order?

_____

_____

_____

_____

_____

_____

3. You

Educative lessons:

- Divine Connection: Recognize that the idea that people are God's servants emphasizes a strong link between people and the greater good. You are encouraged to acknowledge your innate spirituality and your capacity to advance the greater good through this lecture.

- Take time to consider the lessons of humility and surrender. Letting rid of ego-driven ambitions and embracing a willingness to match your actions with divine direction are both essential components of accepting the role of a servant of God.

- Service with Love: Think about how the idea of serving God inspires you to act with love and compassion toward others. This lecture focuses on the idea that actions of service are manifestations of divine love rather than merely jobs.

- Think about how important it is to align your will with the divine will. Alignment with Higher Will. Knowing that you are a servant of God motivates you to look to a higher power for direction and wisdom while making decisions.
- Consider the value of giving oneself to others. Being a servant of God inspires you to put aside your interests and serve and love others in a way that reflects the divine love that permeates you.
- Empowerment through Service: Recognize that accepting the role of a servant of God doesn't lessen your value; rather, it enables you to reach your best potential by utilizing your skills and abilities for the benefit of people everywhere.

Food for thought:

The Wisdom of Surrendering to a Higher Purpose: Think about the lesson of humility and the power of humility. How does realizing "you" as a servant of God encourage you to let go of ego-driven aspirations and follow a path in harmony with divine direction?

_____

_____

_____

_____

_____

_____

Accepting Divine Purpose: Think about the idea of being given a special place in the vast creation. How might realizing that "you" have a mission motivate you to discover your skills and carry out your divine mission?

_____

_____

_____

_____

_____

_____

Consider the relevance of living in harmony with spiritual principles by doing so. How does accepting "you" as God's servant inspire you to exhibit empathy, kindness, and moral conduct in your daily interactions?

_____

_____

_____

_____

_____

_____

Consider the importance of providing others with unselfish service. How does the idea that "you" are God's servant inspire you to live a life of service and generosity that benefits the people around you?

_____

_____

_____

_____

_____

_____

Consider the notions of unity and interconnectedness among all people. How does seeing "you" as a component of a bigger whole motivates you to approach people with compassion, understanding, and a feeling of our shared humanity?

_____

_____

_____

_____

_____

_____

Reflect on the lesson of realizing your inner potential as you are working on unlocking it. How does realizing that "you" is a servant of God inspire you to discover your abilities, passions, and strengths and use them to further your purpose?

_____

_____

_____

_____

_____

_____

Consider the impact of your activities as they spread outward. How may the idea of "you" being a servant of God motivate you to share goodness, love, and transformation with those around you and beyond?

_____

_____

_____

_____

_____

_____

4. Surrender

Educative lessons:

- Developing trust in divine guidance is a necessary part of surrendering to God. Letting go of the demand for total control and allowing yourself to be led by a higher intelligence that understands what is best for your spiritual journey are the lessons to be learned from this experience.

- Release of Ego Attachments: Recognize that submitting necessitates the release of ego-driven attachments. You are urged by this lesson to step back from the results you desire and put more effort into connecting your aspirations to a higher good.

- Accepting Humility: Surrendering to God requires a humble acceptance of your shortcomings. The key takeaway from this experience is that real power comes from accepting humility and realizing that you are part of a greater cosmic order.

- The lesson of achieving peace via surrender is one to be thought about. Giving up personal goals and accepting God's plan can bring about a profound sense of calm and an end to anxiousness.

- Consider the value of releasing resistance before you let it go. When you surrender, you approach life's obstacles with an open heart and a belief that they are opportunities for progress rather than resistance.

- Understanding that surrender doesn't mean giving up your power, but rather that your power is aligned with a higher source, will help you become more empowered. The takeaway is that when you submit, you gain the strength and resilience to face challenges and deal with the complexity of life.

Food for thought:

Consider the idea of having faith in the divine purpose for your life. How does the idea of giving yourself over to God inspire you to relinquish control and believe that the course you're taking is determined by a greater purpose?

_____

_____

_____

_____

_____

_____

Ego Release for Growth: Consider the significance of learning to let go of ego attachments. How may accepting surrender help you let go of ego-driven objectives and make room for your own development and alignment with a greater purpose?

_____

_____

_____

_____

_____

_____

Take into consideration the idea that there is strength in humility. How does giving yourself over to God encourage you to practice humility and admit that giving yourself over to a higher knowledge is where your power lies?

_____

_____

_____

_____

_____

_____

Take into consideration the idea of achieving serenity via surrender. How could submitting to God's will provide you inner peace and release you from the weight of attempting to manage every result?

_____

_____

_____

_____

_____

_____

Consider the value of letting go of resistance when dealing with challenges. How can you approach life's challenges with an open heart, enabling you to overcome obstacles with grace and fortitude, thanks to the act of surrendering?

_____

_____

_____

_____

_____

_____

Alignment in Empowerment: Consider the thought that giving up actually increases your power. How may submitting to God's will genuinely enable you to overcome challenges and realize your potential?

_____

_____

_____

_____

_____

_____

Divine Harmony: Think about how submitting to God puts you in harmony with the divine. In what ways does this idea encourage you to let go of resistance and let life's currents lead you closer to the divine?

_____

_____

_____

_____

_____

_____

5. Miracles

Educative lessons:

- Understand that miracles are frequently considered to be occurrences that go beyond the regular laws of nature. This lesson invites you to consider the notion that a divine power can function outside the bounds of the material universe.

- God's Intervention: Consider the idea of God intervening in your life. The key takeaway from this is to acknowledge that miracles can be viewed as instances of divine intervention that bring about grace, healing, and transformation.

- Change in Perception: Take into account how miracles can cause a change in perception. This lesson challenges you to see tough circumstances through the prism of opportunity and transformation, understanding that miracles can happen even in the middle of struggle.

- Consider the part that faith and belief play in the occurrence of miracles. The takeaway from this is that developing a strong sense of faith and believe in God can lead to amazing experiences that may defy logical explanation.

- Understand that miracles are frequently viewed as expressions of divine love. The point is to reflect on how acts of kindness, love, and compassion might be channels for divine wonders to enter the world.

Food for thought:

Other than Natural Laws: Think about the claim that miracles defy the dictates of nature. How does the idea of miracles inspire you to accept the idea that heavenly forces could be able to act outside the normal bounds of reality?

_____

_____

_____

_____

_____

_____

Consider the idea of divine intervention in your life as evidence of divine presence. How could thinking about miracles lead you to perceive God's presence leading you on your journey through remarkable events?

_____

_____

_____

_____

_____

_____

Consider the lesson of changing your view as you consider your perspective. How can taking into account the occurrence of miracles encourage you to perceive obstacles as chances for development and transformation, enabling you to spot the extraordinary inside the mundane?

_____

_____

_____

_____

_____

_____

Think about how faith and belief affect our ability to see miracles. How does realizing the link between your faith and the occurrence of miracles inspire you to have more faith in the divine order of things?

_____

_____

_____

_____

_____

_____

Take into consideration the concept of co-creating with the divine. How could thinking about miracles inspire you to match your goals and deeds with divine direction, forming a relationship with the miraculous?

_____

_____

_____

_____

_____

_____

Consider the lesson that miracles are frequently manifestations of divine love as you consider miracles as manifestations of love. How does this idea inspire you to consider deeds of kindness and compassion as conduits for the divine to perform its marvels in the world?

_____

_____

_____

_____

_____

_____

Consider the concept of "the miraculous in everyday" and how miracles can be found in mundane situations. How does thinking about miracles motivate you to look for the remarkable in the ordinary and acknowledge the divine presence all around you?

_____

_____

_____

_____

_____

_____

Part II: Practice

6. Relationships

Educative lessons:

- Spiritual development. The takeaway is that through interacting with people, you may assist each other on your individual journeys while also fostering growth for both parties.

- Reflect on how frequently your interpersonal interactions reflect your inner dynamics. Consider how interactions with others might expose aspects of you that require healing, providing an opportunity for self-awareness and change.

- Think on the importance of practicing unconditional love. Relationships in God's eyes inspire you to show compassion and love to people despite their faults, as a reflection of God's perfect love that is incapable of condemnation.

- Consider the ways in which relationships can provide possibilities for forgiveness and healing. Recognize that confrontations can serve as growth accelerators, encouraging you to exercise forgiveness and strive for reconciliation.

- Consider the ways in which relationships illustrate the interdependence of all things. The key takeaway from this is to realize that the connections you have with other people are manifestations of a deeper unity that unites all of humanity.

Food for thought:

Spiritual Development Partners: Think about how connections can aid in your spiritual development. How does the idea of relationships in God's eyes inspire you to uplift your mutual understanding and help one another on their spiritual journeys?

_____

_____

_____

_____

_____

_____

Reflecting Inner Landscape: Consider the notion that your interpersonal interactions reflect your inner dynamics. How might your relationships with others represent aspects of you that are looking for growth and healing, giving you chances to learn more about yourself?

_____

_____

_____

_____

_____

_____

Consider the idea of practicing unconditional love in relationships. Love Beyond Conditions. How can seeing relationships through a divine lens motivate you to show love and compassion to others without placing restrictions on your relationships?

_____

_____

_____

_____

_____

_____

_____

Consider the lesson of forgiveness and interpersonal mending when thinking about renewal. How could conflicts serve as stepping stones to learning how to forgive and aid in the restoration of your relationships?

_____

_____

_____

_____

_____

_____

Consider the idea of supporting one another in relationships. How can sharing your abilities and offering support on each other's travels encourage you to embrace partnerships as means of mutual support?

_____

_____

_____

_____

_____

_____

Think about how relationships can show how intertwined all living things are. How can this viewpoint heighten your awareness of the ties that unite you with others and promote a sense of humanity?

_____

_____

_____

_____

_____

_____

Consider how fostering positive relationships elevates the collective consciousness while talking about elevating the collective. How may exhibiting love, compassion, and understanding in your interactions improve the general well-being of society?

_____

_____

_____

_____

_____

_____

7. Work

Educative lessons:

- Work can be considered a sacred type of contribution, so be aware of that. It is important to understand that your actions in the world have the potential to be significant manifestations of your divine purpose.

- Reflect on the notion that effort can benefit others and the greater good. Consider how you may embody the divine ideal of service by using your professional endeavors to improve the lives of others.

- Aligning with Passion: Take into account the lesson of coordinating your work and passions.

- Integrity and ethics: Consider how work might be carried out with these principles in mind. The lesson here is to approach your pursuits with values that develop honesty and compassion and represent the divine nature inside you.

- The idea of bringing an attentive presence to your work should be considered.
- Consider how cultivating thankfulness and acceptance in your work might help you align with divine principles.

Food for thought:

Purposeful Contribution: Contemplate the idea of work as a purposeful contribution. How does the concept of good works in the sight of God inspire you to approach your tasks with a sense of meaning and intention, recognizing your ability to make a positive impact?

_____

_____

_____

_____

_____

_____

Sacred Service: Reflect on the notion of work as sacred service. How might viewing your work as an opportunity to serve others and align with a higher purpose elevate the quality of your efforts and the impact you create?

_____

_____

_____

_____

_____

_____

Alignment with Values: Consider the lesson of aligning your work with your values. How does the concept of good works encourage you to ensure that your actions and contributions reflect your inner principles and beliefs?

_____

_____

_____

_____

_____

_____

Creating Positive Ripples: Contemplate how your good works can create positive ripples in the world. How might your actions influence others, inspiring them to engage in acts of kindness and service, thereby expanding the circle of goodness?

_____

_____

_____

_____

_____

_____

Contributing to Wholeness: Reflect on how your work contributes to the greater wholeness of humanity. How does the concept of good works in the sight of God remind you that every positive action you take plays a role in bringing greater harmony to the world?

_____

_____

_____

_____

_____

_____

Inspiration through Example: Consider how your commitment to good works can inspire others. How might your dedication to purposeful and meaningful actions serve as an example, encouraging those around you to embody similar values?

_____

_____

_____

_____

_____

_____

8. Body

Educative lessons:

- Recognize that the human body can be thought of as a type of temple for the divine. The moral of the story is to treat your body with respect since it is a sacred medium through which you can communicate with a higher power.

- Consider the value of developing a harmonious relationship between your mind and body.

- Consider the lessons learned through embracing holistic wellness.

- Consider how your body might serve as a channel for acts of kindness and service. The idea here is to comprehend that showing physical kindness to others can be a way to demonstrate your spiritual dedication.

- Consider the idea of transcending bodily material attachments as you think about transcending material attachments.

- Spirituality's Physical Manifestation: Take into account how the treatment of your body reflects your spirituality.

Food for thought:

Temple of Divine Presence: Think about how your behavior is influenced by your perception of your body as a temple of divine presence. How does this viewpoint motivate you to treat your body with respect and care as a vehicle for your spiritual expression?

_____

_____

_____

_____

_____

_____

Reflect on the synergy between your mind and body when you express yourself. How could cultivating a harmonious bond between your thoughts and deeds improve your ability to share divine love and compassion with others?

Consider adopting a holistic approach to well-being when taking care of your body. How does your mental, emotional, and spiritual well-being affect your capacity to exhibit the virtues of devotion and service?

_____

_____

_____

_____

_____

_____

Acts of Compassionate Service: Think about the higher good served by utilizing your body in acts of compassion. How can you use your bodily acts to show those around you God's kindness and love?

_____

_____

_____

_____

_____

_____

_____

Reflect on letting go of physical attachments to your body, such as body image. How could realizing that your body is a temporary container motivate you to change your attention from the physical to the spiritual components of your existence?

_____

_____

_____

_____

_____

_____

Consider how your bodily actions are a tangible manifestation of your spirituality. How does your commitment to living in harmony with divine principles show in the care and mindfulness you provide your body?

_____

_____

_____

_____

_____

_____

Being a Channel: Take into consideration how being a channel for divine expression is made possible by setting aside your body for divine service. How many living from this point of view enable you to manifest divine love and healing through your deeds?

_____

_____

_____

_____

_____

_____

9. Heaven

Educative lessons:

- Heaven can be experienced as a state of inner alignment with love, therefore be aware of this possibility. The lesson here is to understand that the secret to experiencing heaven in your life is to cultivate love, compassion, and kindness inside yourself.

- Transcending Ego: Consider the wisdom in getting beyond ego-driven aspirations.

- Consider the notion of service and giving as passageways to heaven.

- Release of Judgment: Consider the importance of letting go of grudges and judgments.

- Think about the idea of being in harmony with all of creation.

- Think about how important being present and being alert will be when experiencing heaven.

Food for thought:

Inner Love's Direction Think about how your path to paradise is shaped by your alignment with love. How does this idea encourage you to grow in love, compassion, and kindness so that you can ultimately achieve a more paradisiacal existence?

_____

_____

_____

_____

_____

_____

Reflect on the lesson of transcending ego-driven goals in "Transcending Earthly Desires". How many working for heaven help you let go of attachments to things and put your attention on traits that are in tune with the divine?

_____

_____

_____

_____

_____

_____

Consider the idea that serving others and giving to others is a path to heaven. How may your readiness to help others and give of yourself benefit your relationship with the divine and your ascension to heaven?

_____

_____

_____

_____

_____

_____

Take into account the lesson of achieving harmony through forgiving others. How does letting go of grudges and judgments help you to align with the spirit of heaven and foster a peaceful and tranquil environment?

_____

_____

_____

_____

_____

_____

The idea of a single, united humanity should be considered. How may acknowledging the interdependence of all beings and actively seeking to improve the general well-being be a part of the pursuit of heaven?

_____

_____

_____

_____

_____

_____

Consider the significance of mindfulness and presence in achieving heavenly union. How can practicing mindfulness and being fully present in the moment help you connect with the divine energy both within you and all around you?

_____

_____

_____

_____

_____

_____

Consider how your path to paradise is shaped by living by the expression of love. How can seeing heaven both within and around you enable you to embody values of love, compassion, and service?

_____

_____

_____

_____

_____

_____

Self-evaluation Questions:

What new insights have you gained about your relationship with your body, your interactions with others, and your connection to a greater purpose as a result of examining the ideas and principles included in this workbook?

_____

_____

_____

_____

_____

_____

What particular steps or modifications can you make in your daily routine to better reflect the concepts of love, compassion, and service covered in this workbook?

_____

_____

_____

_____

_____

_____

How do your own experiences and personal journeys align with the reflections and insights presented in this workbook? Do any specific incidents or tales leap out to you in particular?

_____

_____

_____

_____

_____

_____

What areas of your life can you strengthen your mindfulness and presence to better care for your well-being, cultivate wholesome relationships, and advance the common good?

_____

_____

_____

_____

_____

_____

Given the continual nature of your exploration and change, how can you use the teachings from this workbook in your continuing spiritual practice and personal growth journey?

_____

_____

_____

_____

_____

_____

Made in the USA
Las Vegas, NV
10 May 2024

89770553R00056